# The Lodge of Washington and his Masonic Neighbors

# Also from Westphalia Press
### westphaliapress.org

# The Lodge of Washington and his Masonic Neighbors

by Charles H. Callahan

New edition introduced by
Paul Rich

WESTPHALIA PRESS
An imprint of Policy Studies Organization

*The Lodge of Washington and his Masonic Neighbors*

**Westphalia Press**
An imprint of Policy Studies Organization
1527 New Hampshire Ave., NW
Washington, D.C. 20036
dgutierrezs@ipsonet.org

**ISBN-13: 978-1935907428**
**ISBN-10: 1935907425**

Cover design by Taillefer Long at Illuminated Stories:
www.illuminatedstories.com

Updated material and comments on this edition
can be found at the Westphalia Press website:
www.westphaliapress.org

A lexandria, Virginia, is rich in Masonic history and has important connections with George Washington. Washington was Worshipful Master of the still extant lodge there, now named Alexandria-Washington Lodge. Washington's family presented the lodge with his wedding gloves, his compass, his pruning knife, and even a piece of the canvas from his tent that he used during the Revolutionary War.

This long out of print introduction to the Masonic aspects of Arlington and the extraordinary connections with Washington's Masonic career offers anecdotes that uniquely add to an appreciation of his life.


Paul Rich
Garfield House, Washington


E

The Lodge of

# WASHINGTON

and his

## MASONIC
## NEIGHBORS

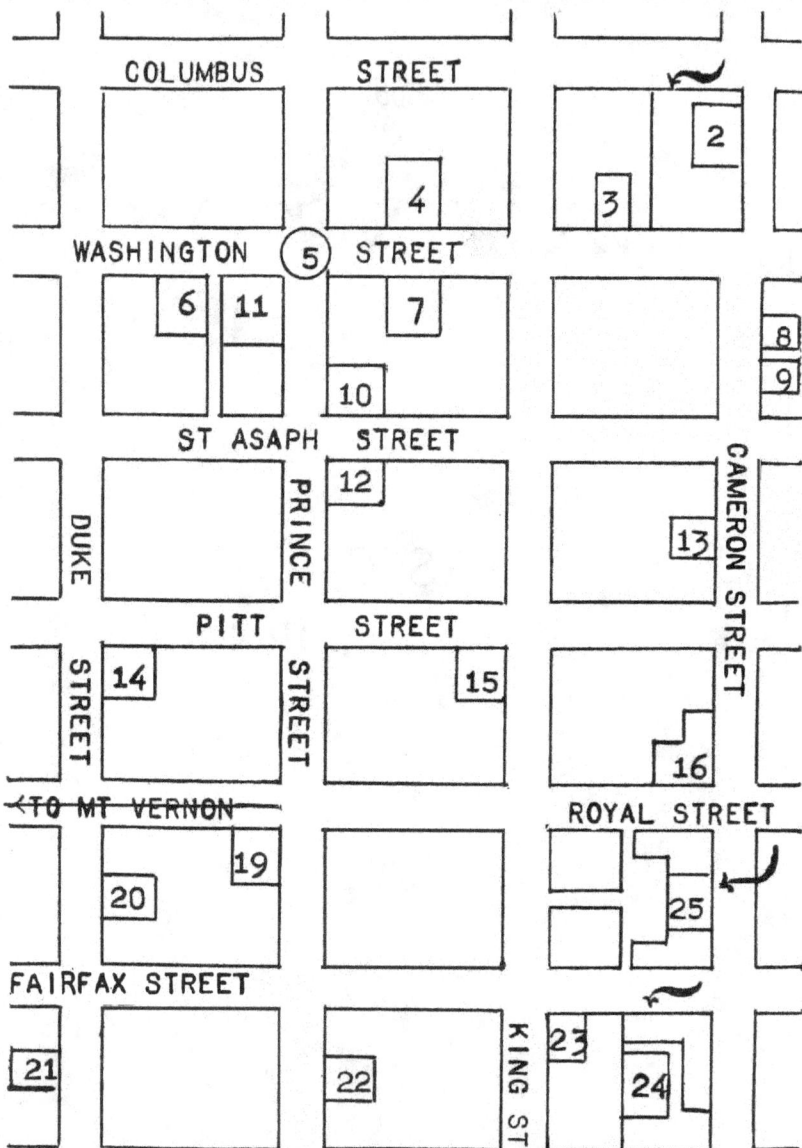

COLUMBUS STREET

WASHINGTON ⑤ STREET

ST ASAPH STREET

PITT STREET

‹TO MT VERNON›

FAIRFAX STREET

ROYAL STREET

DUKE STREET

PRINCE STREET

CAMERON STREET

KING ST

2. Christ Church.
3. M. P. Church.
4. M. E. Church South.
5. Confederate Monument.
6. Baptist Church.
7. Trinity M. E. Church.
8. Gen. Henry Lee's House.
9. Fairfax House.
10. Presbyterian Church.
11. Postoffice.
12. Westminster Building.
13. Washington's Office.
14. St. Paul's Epis. Church.
15. Marshall House.
16. City Hotel.
19. Elk's Hall.
20. Catholic Lyceum.
21. Dr. Craik's House.
22. Dr. Dick's House.
23. Ramsay House.
24. Carlyle House.
25. Masonic Lodge.

# An Appreciation

The collection of heirlooms in Alexandria-Washington Lodge is insignificant in point of numbers and, perhaps, monetary value when compared with other great collections in this and other countries, but owing to the peculiar nature of its acquisition it stands alone in sentimental worth, hallowed by the traditions of a century gone and the fond memories which gather around Washington and his neighbors.

CHARLES H. CALLAHAN.

CITY HALL AND MASONIC TEMPLE. ARROW INDICATES MASONIC TEMPLE

## Alexandria City, Its Location and Environments

LOCATED on the west bank of the Potomac River, six miles south, in plain view, and directly in the line of railroad travel from the National Capital to Mount Vernon, on the public highway, from north to south, a typical colonial town, Alexandria has, with commendable care and pride, preserved its original old-fashioned appearance and delights in its historical associations.

Having been organized in 1749 pursuant to an act of the General Assembly of Virginia, the city is one of the oldest municipalities in the State, and for over half a century was the county seat of Fairfax, in which county Mount Vernon is located, and we find among the Trustees constituting its first legislative body Washington's relatives, patrons and warm personal friends, viz.: Thomas Lord Fairfax, by whom at that time—1749 —the boy was engaged as a surveyor; William Fairfax, at whose home— Belvoir—he had lived while pursuing his studies; George William Fairfax, his preceptor and companion of his first surveys; Lawrence Washington, his half-brother, and John Carlyle, in whose dwelling he was afterwards commissioned a Major on Braddock's Staff, and in 1765 Washington himself was made a member of this famous Town Council, and served as such until the town's incorporation—1779.

From early manhood to venerated age he mingled in social and political intercourse with its people; its representative in the House of Burgesses; vestryman in its old Christ Church; he surveyed its streets, and founded and endowed its first free school. Here, in 1755, he received his commission in the English Army under Braddock; here, to the freeholders of Fairfax County, he first announced his espousal of the cause of the Colonies; here he called, in March, 1785, the Maryland and Virginia Commissioners to confer on boundaries and the rights of import duties and navigation between the two States. This Council adjourned to Mount Vernon, and from there issued an appeal to the several States which resulted in the convention at Philadelphia, 1787, which framed the Constitution of the United States. Here, in 1799, he held his last military review, and cast his last ballot; and here, January 20, 1800, Colonel George Deneale, Master of the Masonic Lodge and Clerk of the Court, recorded his will.

It was the scene of his early social and political triumphs, the starting point of the greatest epochs in his life. Here he conferred with his neighbors on solemn questions of state and determined upon the course of action to pursue.

Its citizens formed his funeral cortege; its soldiers sounded taps and paid the only military tribute at his grave; its ministers conducted his funeral service; its Masons deposited the Apron, Glove and Evergreen on his bier and pronounced its ancient benediction.

OLD LODGE ROOM

East View of Old Alexandria-Washington Lodge, No. 22, A. F. & A. M., Alexandria, Va.
General George Washington, First W. M., 1788

## Alexandria-Washington Lodge, No. 22

ON FEBRUARY 25, 1783, was held the first regular communication of the first Masonic Lodge in this city, instituted by the Provincial Grand Lodge of Pennsylvania; it was known as No. 39 of that Jurisdiction. General Washington was elected an honorary member shortly after his return from the Revolution, and his fondness for the old institution is evidenced by a letter written to the Lodge (see page 15 of this prospectus). After the surrender of the Pennsylvania warrant, application for a new charter was made to the Grand Lodge of Virginia and General Washington became first or charter Master of Alexandria Lodge, No. 22, A. F. & A. M., in 1788, and was subsequently elected to succeed himself, serving in all about twenty months. The instrument containing his name as Master, signed by Edmund Randolph, Governor of the Commonwealth and Grand Master of Masons in Virginia, is still its badge of authority, still hangs on its wall in silent testimony of the love and loyalty of Washington and Randolph for the noble tenets of our institution.

Space will not permit us to even refer to many of the Washington relics in possession of this Lodge. We must content ourselves with brief description of the most interesting and important.

The picture on the opposite page gives the east view of the old Lodge and shows only the Washington Chair, old desk, altar, lesser lights, and the Williams picture of General Washington in Masonic regalia. Fabulous prices have been offered for many of these relics, but presented, as they were, by the relatives and friends of our first Master, the Lodge has rightly refused to even consider the most flattering inducements, preferring to keep them where they were intended to be kept by the donors, for the pride and glory of the fraternity.

The old records, kept now in the vaults of the Citizens' National Bank, are virtually an unbroken chain of historic Masonic events, from 1783 to the present time, stretching over the whole period of our national existence and beyond. Time-faded and worn, they have come down to us with the old charter, through all the civil and military vicissitudes of over a century and a quarter, telling the story of the loyalty to the Craft in the long ago.

Vandal hands have entered now and then to pilfer a name or despoil a page from this dusty treasure, but the vigilant watch of a faithful guard has preserved intact the simple narratives of the most momentous occasions in the history of American Masonry.

We read the fading lines, terse pictures of mighty events, and pause to contemplate the passing scene. Through the deepening twilight of bygone years, we see our fathers fix the boundary line and lay the tablet that marks the Nation's home. We read again and again the simple story of the funeral service and hear whispered from the olden time the last words spoken o'er the bier of Washington, "So mote it be. Amen."

THE WILLIAMS PORTRAIT OF WASHINGTON

## The Williams Picture

O N THE opposite page will be seen a copy of the Williams picture of Washington, which attracts as much attention as any relic in the Lodge. In 1793 the Lodge, by resolution, requested General Washington, then President and living in Philadelphia, to sit for this picture, and after obtaining his consent, employed Williams, of that city, to execute the work. Washington approved the likeness, and late in 1794 it was received from the artist and accepted by the Lodge.

It is a flesh-colored pastel and pronounced by critics of superior quality. It is an entirely different conception from any other painting of the General extant, resembling in cast and feature the original Houdon statue in Richmond, Va., and is the only painting from life showing the General in extreme old age and in Masonic regalia. Having been ordered, received and accepted by the neighbors and Masonic contemporaries of the General, men who knew him intimately and were with him in every walk of his eventful life, who had followed his fortunes and shared his adversities in war, had counseled and supported him in peace, and who, when his labors ended, had sorrowfully laid him to his eternal rest, it is beyond reasonable conception that these men would have foisted on a credulous and confiding posterity a spurious picture of their friend and compatriot.

Numerous flattering offers have not been sufficient inducement for the Lodge to part with this treasure, and while probably sentiment has enhanced its value in the eyes of the Fraternity beyond its intrinsic worth, past association and its Masonic character prevent the possibility of future disposal. However urgent the needs of the Lodge, the Williams picture will be kept in remembrance of that association for generations of Masons yet to come.

The picture is devoid of idealism, the artist's instructions being: "Paint him as he is," and this Mr. Williams appears to have done, bringing out in bold relief several facial marks or blemishes which the General is known to have possessed, and which are shown in a modified form, if at all, by other artists. The disfiguring scar on his left cheek, spoken of by George Washington Parke Custis in his reminiscences, the black mole under his right ear, and the marks of smallpox on his nose and cheeks are all clearly defined and unmistakable, and this fact adds much to the value of the famous pastel and arouses the deepest interest of both historic and art critics.

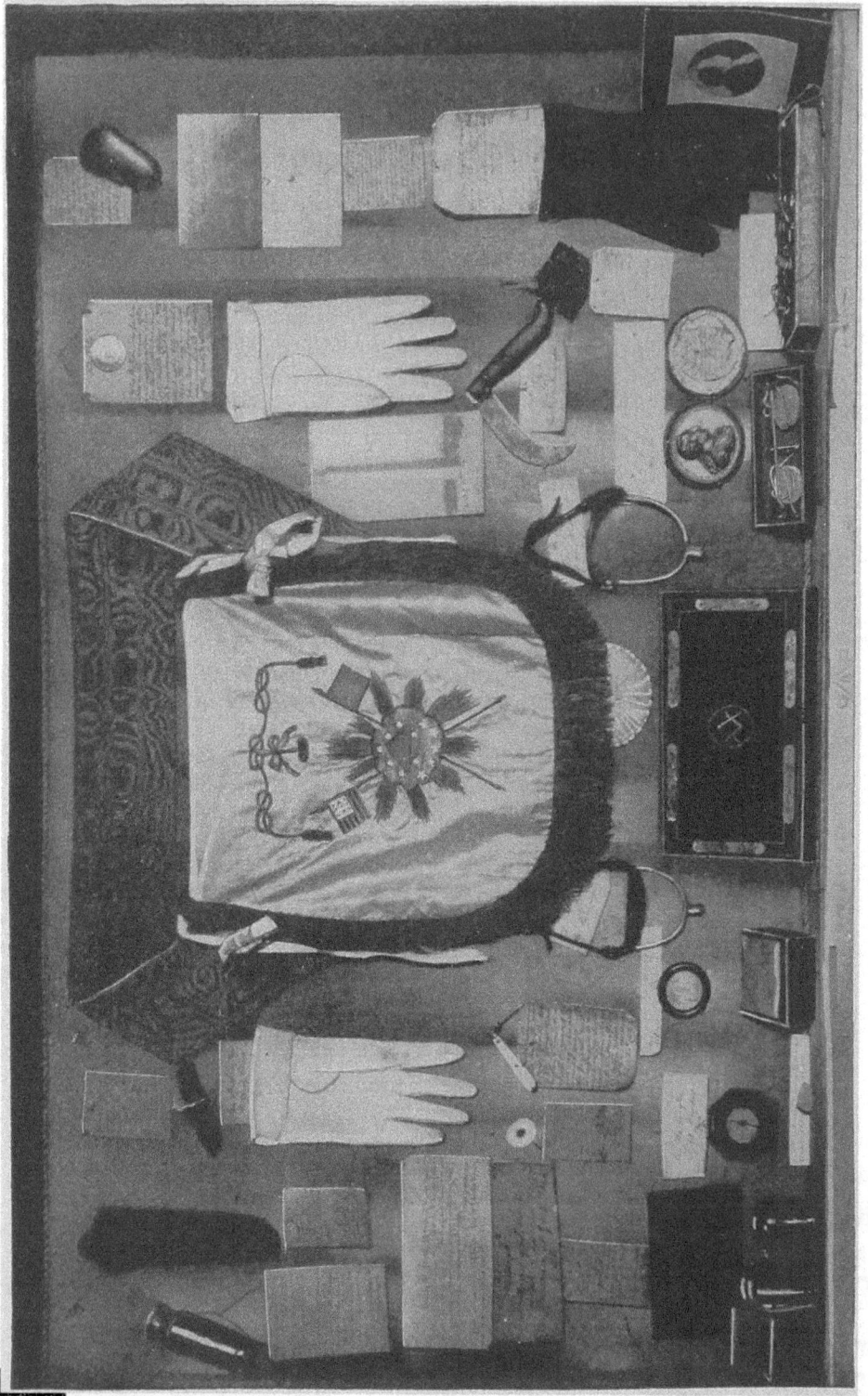

COLLECTION OF PERSONAL EFFECTS OF WASHINGTON

## Group of Relics

THIS COLLECTION, known as "The Washingtonia," contains Washington's Masonic Apron, worn by the General when Master and at laying the corner-stone of the Nation's Capitol. It is of cream-colored satin, heavily fringed and embroidered in gold, with the French and American flags entwined. A beehive and cherubims adorn the center. It was presented to the Lodge with the box below and the sash above in 1812 by Lawrence Lewis, nephew of the General and husband of his adopted daughter, Nellie Custis. The Apron has been seldom worn since the death of the General, among the few instances being by General Lafayette in the Lodge, February 21, 1825; at the laying of the corner-stone of the Washington Monument in 1848; at the laying of the corner-stone of the Yorktown Monument by Grand Master Peyton S. Coles, 1881, and to confer M. M. Degree on Lawrence Washington, February 22, 1910, by the Illinois Delegation. In thanking the Lodge for the use of the Apron at Yorktown, Grand Master Coles wrote in part: "I am deeply gratified by this distinguished honor and in the name of the Grand Lodge, not less than of every individual Mason in the State, I thank you. I count it a high and priceless privilege to be the trusted recipient of so great an honor, and that it has fallen to my humble lot to wear the Masonic clothing, consecrated in our memory by association with Washington and Lafayette, fills me with proud and grateful emotion."

On either side of the Apron are the General's wedding gloves and, beneath, his farm-spurs; to the right, his pruning knife and a black glove worn by the General at his mother's funeral; to the left, a little pearl-handled knife, a present from his mother when a boy (see cut); his pocket compass, cupping and bleeding instruments; a piece of sealing wax taken from his desk after death and last used by the General before dying; boot-strap or garter worn by the General at Braddock's defeat. On the extreme right, near the top, is a copper plate owned and used by John Hancock to print his reception cards while President of the Continental Congress, and presented to General Washington by the Hancock family after the dissolution of the old Colonial Confederacy. These were all given by the General's nephew, Captain George Steptoe Washington, from 1803 to 1812. On the left of the pearl-handled knife is a button, cut from the General's coat at his first inauguration and presented by Doctor James Craik, and to the left of the button, a piece of canvas from his army tent used during the Revolutionary War, presented by George Washington Parke Curtis, his adopted son. In the lower right corner, a picture of Doctor Dick; Doctor Dick's and Washington's medicine scales and a medallion of Washington presented to the General as founder of free schools in Alexandria, Va., by D. Eggleston Lancaster, Esquire, founder of free schools in England, and other relics of importance, which space will not permit to enumerate.

# The Old Clock

THE OLD clock, shown above, was the bedchamber clock of General Washington. On the death of the General, Doctor Elisha Cullen Dick, Master of "No. 22," and one of the attending physicians, cut the pendulum cord and stopped the old timepiece at twenty minutes after ten P.M. After the funeral, Mrs. Washington presented the clock to Doctor Dick for the Lodge. "Its work is done, but the hands still point to the minute and hour that marks the close of the greatest life in history." It is said to be the only piece of furniture in the room at the time of the General's death which has not been restored to its former place. The pendulum with the catgut cord attached is shown to the left of the clock.

## The Lesser Lights

The Lesser Lights in the picture are the original lights of the Lodge and were used on the most important occasions in the history of the institution, among them, laying the corner-stone of the District of Columbia in 1791, the National Capitol in 1793, and the funeral of General Washington in 1799, and at laying the corner-stone of the Washington Monument in 1848.

## The Hour Glass

The hour glass is the original, except one column, which, having been broken, was replaced by a new one and the old column cut in small pieces for souvenirs. It has served as the emblem to teach the sublime lesson of human life from the beginning of the Lodge to the present time.

# The Lodge of Washington

## The Story of the Knife

WHEN George Washington was eleven years old his father died (1743). Shortly after the boy took up his residence at Mount Vernon with his half-brother, Lawrence, and while waiting for repairs to Mount Vernon House stopped at Belvoir, the home of

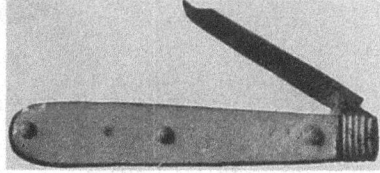

William Fairfax, an intimate friend and neighbor, father-in-law of Lawrence. Through the influence of his brother and the Fairfaxes, he obtained a commission as midshipman in the English Navy. All preparations had been made for his departure, when his mother's message, her final command, forbidding the step, arrived. In obedience to that command and in deference to her wish, the boy surrendered his commission and returned to his studies, back to surveying and mathematics. Among the items of his mother's next order to England, for annual supplies, was one for a good penknife. This she presented to the boy as a reward for his submission to her will, with the injunction, "Always obey your superiors." He carried the token with him through life, as a reminder of his mother's command, and to General Knox explained its significance. At Valley Forge, when a vacillating and timid Congress failed to provide food and shelter for his ragged and starving army, in desperation and despair, yielding temporarily to his feelings and sympathy for his men and in disgust with Congress, he wrote his resignation as Commander-in-Chief, summoned his staff and notified them of his action. Among the officers present and sitting in council was Knox, who reminded him of the story of the knife and his mother's injunction, " 'Always obey your superiors'; you were commanded to lead this army and no one has ordered you to cease leading it." Washington paused, then replied, "There is something in that. I will think it over." Half an hour later he had torn up his resignation, determined to fight on to the end.

Thus upon this slender thread, the story of a little knife and a mother's injunction, hung for one brief moment the future life of a great nation, whose governmental principles have enlightened and elevated humanity. A mother's gentle command determined the course of a noble son and changed the map of the world. The little knife is shown above. It was given the Lodge in 1812 by Captain George Steptoe Washington, a nephew of the General, and one of the executors of his will. The card attached states that it was in Washington's possession about fifty-six years. Partly legendary and partly historical, the narrative, like other tales of his childhood, serves to illustrate the character of the boy and the man and is beautifully told in Owen Wister's "Seven Ages of Washington," page 179.

# Washington's Chair

THE CHAIR occupied by General Washington when Worshipful Master of "No. 22," is shown above. It was in continuous use for 118 years, but as "constant dripping wears the stone," so this old Chippendale, which had borne its precious burden when new and strong, began slowly to yield to the grind of time and usage.

The rips in the seat and arms were, however, the work of vandals, the ever-present and unscrupulous relic-fiend. To preserve it from further abuse, it was placed in a glass case and is not used except on very important occasions.

The frame of mahogany is inlaid with white holly and upholstered in leather. In the course of its long service, many distinguished visitors have occupied it, among them General Lafayette in 1825, President Taft, Vice-Presidents Fairbanks and Marshall, Speaker Cannon, Admiral Schley and others.

Mount Vernon 28th Decr 17??

Gentlemen

       With a pleasing sensibility
I received your favor of the 26th, and
beg leave to offer you my sincere thanks
for the favorable sentiments with
which it abounds. —
       I shall always feel pleasure
when it may be in my power to ren-
der service to Lodge No 39, and in
every act of brotherly kindness to the
members of it; being with great truth
       Your affecte Brother
       and Obedt Servant
       Go Washington

Robt Adam Esqr Master,
& the Wardens & Treasr
    of Lodge No 39.

**LETTER FROM GENERAL WASHINGTON TO LODGE 39**
**(OLD NUMBER OF NO. 22)**

LORD FAIRFAX

## Lord Fairfax

THOMAS, Sixth Lord Fairfax, Baron of Cameron, was born in England (1690) and emigrated to Virginia in 1743. From his mother, daughter of Lord Culpeper, he inherited 5,500,000 acres of land, located between the Potomac and Rappahannock Rivers and extending from the Chesapeake Bay to the Shenandoah Valley. In 1749, with Lawrence Washington, William Fairfax, Gerard Alexander and others, he founded the City of Alexandria, Va., but shortly after this event retired permanently to his estate, Greenway Court, in Frederick

County, whither the boy, George Washington, early in the month of March, 1748, journeyed with George William Fairfax, cousin of the baron, to survey and subdivide the lands of his lordship. Washington was only sixteen years of age, and this was the beginning of his public career and the beginning of the friendship between the mighty lord and youthful surveyor, which lasted unbroken until the death of Fairfax in 1781.

First to discover the elements of greatness in the young pioneer, he lost no opportunity in recommending him to high authorities for positions of trust and responsibility, and to Fairfax, more than any other man, can be accredited the honor of fostering and developing the genius of the precocious youth, whose life is a marvel to mankind and a history within itself. The painting was made in London in 1730 and is the only original picture of the famous old baron extant.

## The Washington Trowel

ON THE front cover is a reproduction of the little trowel used by General Washington, President of the United States, at laying of the corner-stone of the National Capitol, September 18, 1793. The ceremony, briefly described below, marks an epoch in the history of American Masonry, was conducted by the Grand Lodge of Maryland, which at that time and until 1811 held jurisdiction over the present District of Columbia, Right Worshipful Joseph Clarke, Grand Master pro tem., officiating. In the order of procession to the site of the Capitol, President Washington, with Doctor Dick on his right and the Grand Master, pro tem., on his left, marched behind his own Lodge, "No. 22," which acted as escort of honor to the President. On arriving at the site, the column in front inclined two steps, one to the right and one to the left, faced each other, forming a hollow, oblong square, through which the procession filed in reversed order. The President of the United States and Grand Master pro tem., and the Worshipful Master of "No. 22," taking their stand to the east of a large stone and all the Craft forming a circle westward, stood for a short time in solemn order. The Grand Marshal presented to the Commissioners a silver plate appropriately inscribed, which was read and delivered to Washington, who, with the Grand Master pro tem. and the three Worshipful Masters, descended to the cavazion trench and laid it on the corner-stone of the Capitol of the United States.

The trowel is of silver with an ivory handle, was made by John Duffey, a silversmith, who married the daughter of General Washington's landscape gardener. The last important occasion on which it was used was to lay the corner-stone of the George Washington Masonic National Memorial Temple at Alexandria, Va., on November 1, 1923, by Right Worshipful Charles H. Callahan, Grand Master pro tem. of the Grand Lodge of Virginia, assisted by President Coolidge.

EDMUND RANDOLPH

# Edmund Randolph

EDMUND RANDOLPH, whose picture is shown above, had an eventful and interesting life. Born in Williamsburg in 1753, he was disinherited by his father for espousing the cause of the Colonies; became aide to Washington in 1775, Governor of Virginia in 1776-77, member of the convention that framed the Constitution of the United States, and Attorney General and Secretary of War in Washington's Cabinets; was a prominent and active Mason, and as Grand Master of Masons in Virginia in 1788 signed the charter of Alexandria Lodge, No. 22, with General Washington as first Worshipful Master. He died in 1813.

DOCTOR ELISHA CULLEN DICK
(FROM PAINTING IN ALEXANDRIA-WASHINGTON LODGE)

# Doctor Dick

ELISHA CULLEN DICK came to Alexandria from Philadelphia prior to 1783. One of the organizers of the first Lodge, No. 39, he served as Secretary of the first meeting of that Lodge February 25, 1783, and was the last W. M. under the Pennsylvania jurisdiction. In 1789 Dick succeeded General Washington as Master of Lodge No. 22, and as such laid the corner-stone of the District of Columbia in 1791. With his Lodge as escort of honor, he accompanied General Washington and assisted in laying the corner-stone of the National Capitol (1793); was one of the physicians at Washington's bedside when he died; presided at the funeral Lodge called December 16, 1799; was member of the Committee on Arrangements, and performed the Masonic service at his funeral, December 18, 1799. Dick's silk apron, worn at the funeral of Washington, his medicine scales, and some of his medical books are now among the valued possessions of the Lodge. He died in 1828, and is buried in the Quaker Cemetery on Queen Street, Alexandria.

**LAFAYETTE**

(BY CHARLES WILSON PEALE)

## Painting of General Lafayette in
## Washington Lodge

OF ALL the patriotic figures of the Revolution, not one held or deserved to hold a higher place in the esteem and confidence of Washington than the young Marquis de Lafayette. His heroic espousal of the cause of the Colonies, when a mere youth, and a chivalrous resistance of the tyranny and oppression of his native land, have created for him an ideal place in the history of both nations. The painting on the opposite page was executed in 1784, immediately after the Revolutionary War, by Charles Wilson Peale, and presented to the Lodge by an English admirer. It shows the Marquis in the uniform of a Continental General Officer at the age of twenty-seven. In 1824-25 Lafayette visited America for the last time and while on this trip was entertained by Washington Lodge at a called communication held February 21, 1825. In receiving the distinguished guest, Dr. Thomas Semmes, Worshipful Master, addressed him as follows: "You have ever been revered as one of the pillars of our Temple. It affords me inexpressible pleasure to be the organ of my Brethren, here assembled, to welcome you into the bosom of this Lodge, in which your highly valued friend, the beloved 'Father of Our Country,' was wont to preside over our labors and inculcate the principles of our Order, Friendship, Morality, Brotherly Love and Charity. While it is our pride and boast that we had him to rule over us, we also esteem ourselves peculiarly happy in having you for our patron. When Masonry has such supporters, its principles will be maintained, its cause must flourish." To which General Lafayette replied: "Worshipful Sir and Brethren of Washington Lodge, I receive with peculiar sensation this mark of kindness and attention and these expressions of esteem from my Masonic Brethren, and it is particularly gratifying to my feelings to visit the Lodge over which our lamented illustrious Brother Washington presided. I shall ever cherish a high regard for Masonry and pray you, Worshipful Sir, and the rest of the Brethren, to accept my particular and grateful acknowledgment." On this occasion Lafayette presented the Lodge with the front door key of the Bastile, which, made by hand of wrought iron, weighs five pounds, a striking reminder of that house of horrors. The key with a silk sash containing the picture of Lafayette, worn by him in the Lodge on the occasion of his visit, is now kept in a glass case for security and protection. It would be interesting, if space permitted, to give the full account (still preserved among our old records) of this visit of Lafayette to the Lodge, the many pleasant and beautiful expressions of friendship and affection paid the gallant and now venerable Frenchman by his Revolutionary compatriots, who gathered for the last time to review the scenes of former struggles in the cause of American Independence. Lafayette was made an Honorary Member of the Lodge at this meeting.

PRESENT LODGE ROOM

**DR. JAMES CRAIK**
(FROM A PAINTING IN ALEXANDRIA-WASHINGTON LODGE)

# Dr. James Craik

D R. JAMES CRAIK was born near Dumfries, Scotland, 1730, and emigrated to America in 1750; was surgeon in Washington's first command and with him in the Battle of the Great Meadows, 1754. For gallant conduct and meritorious service at the Battle of Monongahela, 1755, Craik was officially commended. In 1760 he married Washington's cousin, Mariamne, daughter of Charles Ewell, of Belle Air, Prince William County, Va. He was Surgeon-General in the Continental Army and Director of the Hospital at Yorktown. He was perhaps the most intimate friend of Washington, who refers to him in his will as "My old and intimate friend, Dr. Craik." Was with the General in every battle he fought, from Great Meadows to Yorktown. He ministered to the dying Braddock at Monongahela, and saw the gallant Hugh Mercer breathe his last on the field of Princeton; dressed Lafayette's wounds at Brandywine; was at the death bed of John Custis—Mrs. Washington's son—at Eltham, after Yorktown; with Washington when he passed to the great beyond, and soothed the dying moments of Martha, the wife of Washington. Dr. Craik died at Vauclause, near Alexandria, February 5, 1814, in the 84th year of his age, and was interred in the burial grounds of the old Presbyterian Meeting House on South Fairfax Street, Alexandria.

## Nellie Custis

THIS PICTURE of Eleanor (Nellie) Custis, adopted daughter of Washington and grand-daughter of his wife, Martha, is from a painting in Alexandria-Washington Lodge; but the reproduction fails to do full justice to either the subject or the painting from which it was taken. This, however, seems to be unavoidable, as the canvas was badly injured when the old Temple was burned in 1871. On the death of her father, John Custis, son of Mrs. Washington, November 5, 1781, General Washington adopted his two youngest children—Nellie and George Washington Parke Custis. These children were reared at Mount Vernon, and on the 22d of February, 1798, Nellie married Major Lawrence Lewis, Washington's nephew and Social Secretary. After the death of the General, Mrs. Lewis and husband erected Woodlawn, about three miles inland from Mount Vernon, and on a part of that estate which she had inherited from the General. She died in 1852, and is buried beside the tomb at Mount Vernon. Woodlawn is still standing.

(FROM A PAINTING IN
ALEXANDRIA-WASHINGTON LODGE)

## Miss Betsy Fauntleroy

NUMEROUS writers have endeavored to weave around the youth of Washington the halo of romance, and have connected his name in a sentimental way with a number of the leading belles of Colonial times. In boyhood letters he speaks forlornly of his "Lowland Beauty." Who was the "Lowland Beauty?" She has been variously identified as Miss Mary Cary, Miss Lucy Grimes, and others; but the following letter, written to William Fauntleroy, Esquire, of Naylors Hole, on the Rappahannock River, in 1752, and unearthed by General Fitzhugh Lee, lends color to the claim that Betsy Fauntleroy was this lady of mystery:

"May 20, 1752.

"To Wm. Fauntleroy, Sr.

"Sir: I should have been down long before this, but my business in Frederick detained me somewhat longer than I expected and immediately upon my return from thence, I was taken with a violent pleurice which has reduced me very low; but propose, as soon as I recover my strength, to wait on Miss Betsy in hopes of revocation of the former cruel sentence, and see if I can meet with any alteration in my favor. I have enclosed a letter to her, which should be much obliged to you for the delivery of it. I have nothing to add but my best respects to your good lady and family.

"GEO. WASHINGTON."

25

THE FLAG OF WASHINGTON'S BODYGUARD

# The Lodge of Washington

## The Flag Borne by Washington's Bodyguard

IN 1871 a disastrous fire not only destroyed the old temple erected by Washington's contemporaries in 1802 but the entire City Hall as well. At that time, 1871, as now, the most valuable relics were kept in the Lodge Room, but as early as 1818 the collection had grown so large that the City Council provided a room in the City Hall, adjoining the Lodge for the accommodation of the overflow and gave it the name of Alexandria-Washington Lodge Museum. The major portion of the relics retained in the Lodge Room were rescued, but a large number deposited in the Museum were either destroyed or disappeared after the fire, and a partial list of these is given on the following page, some of which have been since returned.

After the fire the relics and furniture were deposited in the basement of a local printing office operated by Robert Bell & Sons, where they remained until the completion of the new temple in 1873, when they were returned to the Lodge Room, where they have since remained. Among the valued possessions supposed to be lost and so catalogued were a number of flags of the Revolutionary period. In the Fall of 1926 the Bell Printing establishment, in the basement of which the property of the Lodge had been stored, changed hands, and Mrs. Ola V. Bell, widow of one of the former proprietors who was a member of the Lodge, in renovating the premises discovered four of the long lost banners and promptly restored them to the Lodge authorities.

Amongst these was the emblem of Washington's Bodyguard shown on the opposite page. Washington's Bodyguard was composed of about two hundred and fifty selected men who were retained at headquarters for special service such as secretaries, aides de camp, etc., to the Commander in Chief, and other duties of an important nature. The contingent was in command of Capt. Caleb Gibbs, and among the officers was Washington's nephew, Lieut. George Lewis, son of his sister Betty.

The other three flags found and returned by Mrs. Bell were the flag of the Independent Blues of Alexandria, carried by that company in the Revolution, at Washington's funeral and in the War of 1812; the flag of the Alexandria Riflemen, Company No. 2, of the celebrated Daniel Morgan's Regiment of Riflemen; and a large banner inscribed "The LaFayette Flag." The three last mentioned banners have not as yet been restored, but efforts are being made to that end. After their restoration they will be immediately put on exhibition.

# The Lodge of Washington

## Partial List of Relics Lost in Fire of 1871

At the time of its destruction the Museum had been in existence for a period of sixty years, and was a great resort for strangers visiting the town.

Among the relics and other articles of value destroyed were:

The bier upon which the remains of Washington were borne to the tomb, and the crape that floated from the door of his home to tell the sad news of his death.

A picture of Martha, the wife of Washington, in her youthful days.

A portrait of Washington.

Washington's military saddle.

Portions of a "settee" of Washington, which once stood in the hall of the old Mount Vernon Mansion.

Washington's card tables.

Many original letters of Washington in frames.

A flag used by an Alexandria company in the Revolution—a faded red, with yellow center, inscribed in black: "IX Virginia Regiment, Alexandria Company"; staff wood, stained red, with wooden lance.

The flag of Washington's life-guard. (See pages 26, 27.)

The flag of the Richmond Rifle Rangers in the Revolution—white silk, elegantly painted, with a device-motto: "Nemo me impune lacessit."

A leather satchel, similar to a soldier's haversack, said to have been carried by Mustapha Pasha, Dey of Algiers, during his pilgrimage to the tomb of Mahomet.

A bust of the celebrated John Paul Jones, which was presented to Washington by Lafayette, and adorned the dining-room at Mount Vernon.

A number of portraits, which adorned the walls, and among others, that of William Penn, by West.

The flag of the Independent Blues, of Alexandria, used in the war of 1812-1814.

The flag used by Paul Jones on the "Bon Homme Richard."

A portrait of Lafayette.

The model of the first French guillotine, which recalled all the horrors of the bloody bygone days, when even rulers trembled on their thrones for fear of its tortures.

The dagger with which the Bey of Tunis was killed.

One of the candles used at the mass before the execution of Louis XIV.

A saddle of crimson velvet, heavily embroidered with gold, sent as a present to Thomas Jefferson by the Dey of Morocco.

The model of a corn-planter, invented by George Washington Parke Custis, 1790.

The model of the Triumphal Arch through which Lafayette rode at Alexandria, on his reception by the citizens on Saturday, October 16, 1824, and a stuffed eagle which was, in life, perched on the top of it.

OLD TOMB

# Funeral of Washington

GENERAL GEORGE WASHINGTON died at Mount Vernon twenty minutes after ten o'clock P. M., Saturday, December 14, 1799, and his body was deposited in the Old Tomb, shown above, at a few minutes after three P. M., on Wednesday, December 18. Libelous or ignorant sceptics, the enemies of our institution, have denied that Washington received Masonic burial, in an official sense, or that he was even a Mason, in good standing, at the time of his death. In order that every member of the American Craft may know the true story of the funeral and form his own conclusions, we will draw from the old minutes of "No. 22" for our account of this imposing ceremony.

In attendance at the bedside of the General in his last illness and when he expired were three physicians, namely, Doctors Dick, Craik and Brown, all of whom were Masons. The first two were members of Washington's own Lodge, "No. 22," Doctor Dick being Master, and Dr. Brown was the 5th Grand Master of Maryland. On Monday, the 16th of December, 1799, to make arrangements for the interment, a funeral Lodge was called, Doctor Dick presiding, with Colonel George Deneale, Senior Warden pro tem., and Colonel Dennis Ramsay, Junior Warden pro tem. In conformity to the plan agreed upon at this communication, at an early hour on the following Wednesday, December 18, the Lodge and visiting Brethren, under escort of the militia and citizens of Alexandria, started for Mount Vernon, where they arrived about one o'clock P. M. The funeral procession being formed, moved in the following order: First, the troops, horse and foot; next, the clergy, Reverends James Muir, Thomas Davis, William Maffit, and William Addison, the first three being members of "No. 22." The General's horse, with saddle, holsters and pistols, led by two grooms, Cyrus and Wilson; music; guard of honor; then the bier, borne by four young Lieutenants of the "106th Regiment of Virginia Militia," namely Lawrence Hooff, Jr., James Turner, George Wise and William Moss; pallbearers, Colonel Charles Simms, Dennis Ramsay, William Payne, George Gilpin, Charles Little and Philip Marsteller, all Revolutionary officers and all members of "No. 22," except Colonel Marsteller, who was not a Mason, but whose son, Philip, was, and was present with the Lodge. Next came the mourners and then the Masons, seventy-nine in all. Colonel George Deneale, Junior Warden, commanding the troops, Captain Piercy, Senior Warden, commanding his company, the "Alexandria Blues," Captain Young, a member, the cavalry, and Captain William Harper, also a member, the artillery. On arriving at the tomb, the services of the Episcopal Church were performed by Reverend Thomas Davis, Rector of Christ Church, and member of the Lodge, and the Masonic service by Doctor Elisha C. Dick, Worshipful Master of "No. 22," assisted by Reverend James Muir, Chaplain.

It can be seen from this brief abstract, the full text of which is given in the "History of the Lodge of Washington," and in Hayden's "Washington and His Masonic Compeers," both accounts corresponding to the old minutes of "No. 22," how essentially Masonic in all its details was the funeral of Washington, the greatest of all Americans, and how little importance has been attached to this imposing event, in the history of our country, even by zealous Masonic writers of careful research and wide renown. To Hayden, therefore, more than any other man, are we indebted for the full account of the ceremonies, who, when compiling his splendid work, quoted above, away back in the "fifties," took the trouble to examine carefully the old minutes of "No. 22" and obtain the data which formed the basis of his excellent description of this important event.

The route pursued by this funeral Lodge to and from Mount Vernon, a distance of about nine miles, was in that day a primitive highway and required several hours of tedious and laborious effort to make the journey. The sun had already sunk behind the western hills, and the gathering shadows had begun to fall when the sad procession resumed its homeward journey. Although the list of those participating in this historic event has frequently been published, it will perhaps be not amiss to chronicle their names again. Indeed, it may be that some reader of this little booklet will find among the devoted band of Masons the familiar name of a cherished ancestor:

# The Lodge of Washington

Dr. Elisha Cullen Dick, Worshipful Master
Henry Piercy, Senior Warden
George Deneale, Junior Warden
David Wilson Scott, Secretary
Robert B. Jamesson, Treasurer
William Bartleman, Senior Deacon
Josiah Faxson, Junior Deacon
John C. Kempff, Tiler

Colonel Charles Simms
Colonel Dennis Ramsay
Colonel William Payne
Rev. Dr. James Muir
Rev. William Maffit
Dr. James Gillis
William Ramsay
John McKnight
Peter Cottom
Forrest Richardson
Joseph Neale
Thomas Peterkin
Charles Turner
James MacKenzie
Joseph Thomas
Jonathan Swift
Ferdinando Fairfax
Wm. Byrd Page
Philip G. Marsteller
Robert Young
William Hodgson
Joseph Gilpin
Dr. Augustine J. Smith
John Borrowdale
Thomas Rogerson
Robert Patton
Baldwin Dade
Charles Alexander
John 'C. Hunter
Philip Dawe
John Kincaid
John Muir
Alexander Latimer
James D. Wescott
Patrick Byrne
John Williams
James Hays

Colonel George Gilpin
Colonel Charles Little
Dr. James Craik
Rev. Thomas Davis
Captain William Harper
George Graham
William Johnston
Guy Atkinson
John T. Brooks
Michael Flannery
Dennis McCarty Johnson
Joshua Riddle
George Coryell
Alexander MacKenzie
George Chapman, Jr.
Bernard Ghequiere
John McIver
William Herbert
James Wilson
Richard Conway
Walter Jones, Jr.
Thomas Triplett
Robert Alexander
Robert Allison
Mark Butts
Philip Magruder
William Jackson
Stephen Stephens
David Martin
Charles Jones
Robert Brocket, Sr.
John Lemoine
James Davidson
James Wigginton
John Bogue
George Lane

31

CHRIST CHURCH, ALEXANDRIA, VA.

# Christ Church

BEFORE the Revolution General Washington usually attended Pohick Church in Fairfax County, about seven miles below Mount Vernon, but upon the completion of Christ Church in Alexandria in 1773, he purchased a pew in that house of worship, for which he paid the sum of 36 pounds and 10 shillings, and after that time, when at home, was a regular attendant at this church. In it, in 1853, Robert E. Lee, the great Southern leader, was confirmed in the Episcopal faith by the renowned Rev. John Johns, afterwards Bishop of the Diocese of Virginia. The interior of the church has been changed several times, but the pew of Washington has been restored to its original design, and both the pews of Washington and Lee are marked. The present gallery was erected in 1787, and the steeple was added in 1818. Some of the most eminent divines in Virginia have served as Rectors of this parish, among them Bryan, the Eighth Lord Fairfax, David Griffith, William Meade, and Randolph McKim, and on the vestry register we find, in addition to General Washington, the names of Lord Bryan Fairfax, Ludwell Lee, Edmund I. Lee, Captain William Payne, Colonel Charles Simms, Cassius F. Lee, Colonel John A. Washington and General John Mason. The old edifice is redolent with the spirit of sacred history and tradition and is beautifully situated in the heart of the city.

CITY HOTEL, ALEXANDRIA, VA.

# City Hotel

THE CITY HOTEL, formerly Gadsby's Tavern, is full of historic interest. The smaller of the two buildings shown in the picture was, on two occasions, the headquarters of General Washington. While quartered in this building he recruited his first command in 1754, and from there started on his march which resulted in the Battle of Great Meadows. One year later he occupied the same building when made a Major on Braddock's Staff. From the steps of the main or larger building he announced to the assembled throng the result of the convention in Richmond which adopted the Federal Constitution in 1788. From the doorway, in 1789, he delivered a farewell address to his neighbors while on his way to his first inauguration, and from the same steps only a few weeks before he died he reviewed the local troops and gave his last military command. In it the celebrated assemblies, or dances, which Washington and his wife were accustomed to attend, were held. The old ballroom is still to be seen on the second floor of the north section, with its music gallery intact.* In this, the corner building, Paul Jones and Lafayette first met and became acquainted, and it was there that Lafayette was entertained by the Commonalty during his stay in Alexandria while on his last visit to America in 1824. There, in 1798, was held the first celebration of General Washington's birthday, and among those participating were the General and his wife.

*Since the above was written the music gallery has been removed to the Metropolitan Museum of Art in New York City.

CARLYLE HOUSE, ALEXANDRIA, VA.

# Carlyle House

JOHN CARLYLE was of Scotch descent; emigrated to America in 1740; settled in this city about 1744; married Sarah, daughter of William Fairfax, of Belvoir, near Mount Vernon. In 1752 he erected the now famous Carlyle House in Alexandria. The house was occupied in 1755 by General Braddock as his headquarters. It was in this private residence that the famous Council of Governors, consisting of Shirley of Massachusetts, DeLancey of New York, Sharp of Maryland, Morris of Pennsylvania, and Dinwiddie of Virginia, assembled in 1755 to deliberate upon Braddock's campaign at the beginning of the French and Indian War, during which the youthful Washington was made a Major on Braddock's Staff. In it also at this time was made the first suggestion of Colonial taxation by the English Parliament. The picture shows the old mansion as it was before the erection of the buildings which now obscure it from the street. In the building on the corner, to the north of the Carlyle House, was established the first U. S. sub-post office in the United States, and in the basement of this building, the windows of which are protected by iron bars, was established in 1792, with William Herbert, son-in-law of John Carlyle, as President, the Bank of Alexandria, the first chartered institution of its kind in the State of Virginia.

MARSHALL HOUSE, ALEXANDRIA, VA.

# The Marshall House

ON THE southeast corner of King and Pitt Streets is located the Marshall House, formerly occupied as a hotel, and in which was shed the first blood in Virginia during the Civil War. It was in this building on May 24, 1861, that Colonel Ellsworth, of the New York Zouaves, met his death at the hands of James Jackson, the proprietor, who in turn was shot down and bayonetted to death by Francis E. Brownwell and other members of the squad. Jackson had hoisted a Confederate flag over his hostelry and had declared "that the man who lowered it would do so over his dead body." The emblem could be seen with glasses from the heights and roofs of public buildings in Washington, and doubtless Colonel Ellsworth had heard of the incident before landing in Alexandria. Colonel Ellsworth, with his New York Zouaves, came down the Potomac on barges, landing at the foot of Cameron Street. He conducted a small guard or squadron to the scene of the sad and useless tragedy. The entire incident was over in ten minutes after the troops reached the building, but it left heartburns which lasted for years.

ALEXANDRIA ACADEMY, ALEXANDRIA, VA.

# Alexandria Academy

IN THE building shown above, which is still occupied as a public school, General Washington established the first permanent free school in Alexandria. It was attached to, and placed under the supervision of the trustees of what was then known as the Alexandria Academy. The entire correspondence relating to the subject between General Washington and the trustees of the Academy is still extant and a part of the public school record of this city. The General guarantees the annual payment of 50 pounds sterling to maintain a school for the children of indigent people, and a sufficient endowment fund to yield this amount after his death. And in his will can be found this item: "I give and bequeath to the trustees of the Alexandria Academy in the town of Alexandria $4,000.00, or in other words twenty of the shares I hold in the Bank of Alexandria, towards the support of a free school, established at, and annexed to, the said Academy." In 1811 General Henry (Light Horse Harry) Lee moved from Stradford House in Westmoreland County, Va., with his family to this city, and placed his children in the Alexandria Academy, and it was in this old structure that Robert E. Lee of immortal fame received his primary education under the famous Irish pedagogue, Wm. B. Leary. The old house is located in the southern section of the city, on the southeast corner of Wolf and Washington Streets.

WASHINGTON'S TOWN OFFICE, ALEXANDRIA, VA.

## Washington's Town Office

GENERAL WASHINGTON maintained an office in Alexandria, and when at Mount Vernon retained a clerk there. The duties of this Alexandria secretary were to look after the General's local interests, to accommodate belated visitors on their way to Mount Vernon, and give them such attention as their circumstances might require. In October, 1785, George A. Washington, nephew of the General, and a great favorite, married Fannie Bassett, a niece of Mrs. Washington. The young couple made their home at Mount Vernon until after the death of her husband (which occurred while the General was serving his second term as President, and residing in Philadelphia), when the widow, Mrs. Fannie Washington, moved to Alexandria, and occupied the little building shown above until her marriage to Colonel Tobias Lear, Washington's private secretary, after which they made their home at Wellington, about three miles below Alexandria. The building was torn down in 1857, and the picture is all that remains of what would be now an object of historic interest. The building was located on the south side of Cameron Street, between Pitt and St. Asaph Streets.

THE MEMORIAL TO WASHINGTON THE MASON

## The Memorial to Washington the Mason

THE movement to erect a Memorial to Washington as a Mason was conceived by Alexandria-Washington Lodge in 1909, and in the fall of that year invitations were extended to the several Grand Masters in the United States to attend a conference to be held in the Lodge Room on the 22nd of February, 1910. In compliance with this invitation eighteen Grand Masters or their representatives assembled at the appointed time and place and, after considering the proposal of the Lodge, resolved to organize a National Masonic Association for the purpose at hand. Pursuant to these arrangements, a permanent organization was effected on the 22nd of February, 1911. In due course of time a proper site was acquired on Shooters Hill, an elevated plain in the western section of the city. Plans and specifications were adopted, and on June 5, 1922, ground was broken and the work of construction started. On November 1, 1923, the cornerstone was laid with Masonic ceremonies in the presence of one of the largest gatherings of Masons ever assembled on this Continent.

The temple building faces the east and is approached by seven terraces. The main building is 177 feet 8 inches wide by 195 feet 8 inches long, with a semicircular projection in the rear on a radius of 53 feet 10 inches, making the length over all 248 feet 11 inches. The extreme width of the top terrace around the building is 230 feet wide by 300 feet in length and 127 feet above sea level. This terrace is approached by thirty-nine steps 108 feet long. The main building rises 50 feet above the top terrace or 177 feet above tidewater. The tower is divided in five terraces with a total height of 261 feet above the main building, or a total height above sea level of 438 feet.

The structure rests on a solid mat, which covers the entire area of the building and contains approximately 9,000 cubic yards of concrete and 720 tons of reinforcing steel. The total amount of concrete in the foundation, walls and approaches is 16,000 cubic yards. The building above the foundation walls is to be constructed of New Hampshire Conway pink granite, and the entire cost, including landscape decorations, will be approximately $5,000,000, which is to be raised by popular subscription among the individual Masons and Masonic bodies of America. The building will contain, when completed, in addition to Memorial Hall, an auditorium with a seating capacity of one thousand to twelve hundred, executive offices, a replica of old Alexandria-Washington Lodge, which was erected immediately after Washington's death by his contemporaries and destroyed by fire in 1871, Blue Lodge and a composite room for other Masonic Bodies, an assembly hall, a library, museum and art gallery.

## Old Presbyterian Meeting House

THE OLD Presbyterian Meeting House was erected in 1774, partially destroyed by fire in 1836, and rebuilt on the same walls in the same year. In this building the Masons of Alexandria held their first religious ceremony on the anniversary of Saint John the Evangelist in 1783. Its Pastor, the Reverend James Muir, was for years Chaplain of Alexandria-Washington Lodge No. 22 and, as such, performed the religious service of the Lodge at Washington's funeral. Here on December 27, 1799, a memorial service was held and the first eulogy on the departed Washington delivered by the Reverend Mr. Muir. On the following Sunday, December 29, in this building union memorial sermons were preached by the Reverend Thomas Davis of Christ Episcopal Church in the morning and in the afternoon by the Reverend James Muir, Pastor. Here, too, on the 22nd of February, 1800, Dr. Elisha Cullen Dick, Master of Lodge No. 22, delivered an oration on Washington as a Mason in which appears "his fair fame secure in its immortality should shine through countless ages with undiminished luster. It shall be the statesman's polar star, the hero's destiny, the boast of the aged, the companion of maturity and the goal of youth." In the little cemetery surrounding the Meeting House over thirty Revolutionary patriots lie buried, among them Dr. James Craik, Surgeon General of the Continental Army, family physician of Washington and member of Lodge No. 22; Col. Dennis Ramsay, Masonic pallbearer at Washington's funeral and officer of the Lodge; John Carlyle, and other prominent heroes. Here, too, lies buried the "unknown soldier" of the Revolution, whose grave has been recently marked.

www.ingramcontent.com/pod-product-compliance
Lightning Source LLC
Chambersburg PA
CBHW060658280326
41933CB00012B/2230